How to Teach

10 quick lessons for getting an A+ in teaching

Deborah K. Orlik

Marlen Hill Publishing • La Cañada • California

for the children

Published by:
Marlen Hill Publishing
2222 Foothill Blvd. #E314
La Cañada, California 91011-1456

Library of Congress Catalog Card Number: 97-93855
Orlik, Deborah K.
    How to Teach: 10 quick lessons for getting an A+ in teaching

ISBN 0-9633276-7-4
1. Teaching--United States   I. Title
2. Education
3. Children--Education
4. Adult Education--Teaching

Contents

The Beginning

The Beginning

So. You've been asked to teach.

Whether you know it or not, you have been rewarded for something good you must have done.

Teaching is more fun and more rewarding than any other occupation in the world! To study and prepare for class is both interesting and exciting; to watch your students learn is the ultimate satisfaction. Class discussions can provide fascinating insights into our fellow human beings. Testing can be easy. Your job as the guide into unexplained territory can be an inspiration to both you and the students.

This book is designed to get you prepared, to show you how to be a good teacher, self-confident and well-liked, so that you enjoy teaching and your students enjoy learning. That's the goal.

The beginning is easy:

Lesson #1: The good teacher is polite, respectful, sincere, kind, cheerful and fair.

The Teacher You Want To Be

The Goals of Teaching

The most challenging part of teaching is also, of course, the most rewarding. Teaching isn't the process of giving information. Teaching is giving the students the tools to learn how to think for themselves. The good teacher teaches the student:

- self-direction (the ability to set goals)
- self-determination (the ability to act without external compulsion)[1]
- self-control (discipline)
- self-evaluation (reflection and praise)
- self-esteem (which brings with it tolerance, empathy, and the benefits of service to others) and, of course,
- critical thinking[2]

You cannot be with your students throughout their lives so you must teach the students how to set their own goals, analyze problems, and find solutions. You are not teaching just the subject you were assigned to teach; you are giving the students the tools they need to succeed in life.

---

[1] In the vernacular, a self-starter.

[2] Also known as reflective thinking, critical thinking is the process of analyzing a problem, breaking it down into sub-parts, applying knowledge to it, and reaching a conclusion or solution.

Because every person is different, your goal (teaching all of these things to many different people) will only be accomplished through the use of many different teaching techniques and approaches. Listening to each student will help you know how best to let that student learn. The learners must learn for themselves. You can teach your subject, but you must give them the tools that will allow them to learn on their own.

Learning can and should be fun. When we are enjoying the experience, we learn more and retain what we learn longer. When you have mastered all of the "lessons" in this book, you'll be a good teacher who has fun teaching and whose students have fun learning. This is true no matter what age group you teach and whether you teach for a living or live to teach. If you are a full time teacher, there is something in here for you. If you think you are a one-time presenter, once you experience the exhilaration of teaching, you won't be able to get enough of it. When people learn how to learn from you, you will experience the most powerful feeling in the world: the power to improve other people's lives.

Lesson #2: The good teacher shows the student how to learn.

The Self-Confident Teacher

If you are a new teacher or you will be teaching a new subject, you are probably ill-at-ease about teaching. Students like and respect the self-confident teacher. The self-confident teacher is well-prepared in the discipline and well-prepared for each lesson. The self-confident teacher respects the students' views, welcomes questions and listens carefully to students. This teacher seeks help when it is needed. The self-confident teacher is organized. Who needs the teacher who runs into the classroom, sheaves of paper flying, and spends the first five minutes of class getting ready to teach?

You want to get your teaching career and each new semester or school year off to a good start. Begin by getting a three ring binder and arranging your class rules, goals, lesson plans, class assignments, notes and exams in the order in which you will need them for class.

Your first meeting with your students is the most important because, as the saying goes, first impressions are hard to change. You want to be confident on the first day of class and every day thereafter.

Lesson #3: The good teacher is self-confident.

The Well-Liked Teacher

There is nothing wrong with being well-liked. In fact, it's a great feeling. It is easy to be a well-liked teacher. Our first premise (the good teacher is polite, respectful, sincere, kind, cheerful and fair) is an important first step to being well-liked.

The well-liked teacher is the teacher the students recommend to other students. You remember this from when you were in school: "Take Ms. Beach for Intro. to Botany. She's really cool." "Stay away from Mr. Tyler. He is (arrogant, boring...fill in your own adjective)." You want to be like Ms. Beach. You want students standing in line to get into your class.

For the teacher, well-liked is different from being an "easy grader." If the teacher was a jerk, how much did you care that the grades were high? What was the price you paid?

Well-liked is different from being "chummy." Even though your students may be in your age group, you do not want to be pals with them while they are your students. You want to be a good teacher; the "good friends" relationship can wait until after you are no longer the teacher.

Students today want all of the things you wanted when you were in school. You wanted your teachers to be polite, to treat you with respect, to be sincere, kind, cheerful and fair with you. (Lesson 1) You wanted teachers who showed you how to learn on your own. (Lesson 2) You also wanted self-confident teachers who had control of the classroom. (Lesson 3)

Additionally, students want these things in teachers:

Lesson 5:   set fair goals, give encouragement and praise
Lesson 6:   give the opportunity to express and defend positions
Lesson 7:   be prepared and enthusiastic
Lesson 8:   listen to the students
Lesson 9:   be honest
Lesson 10: be creative

After ten years of teaching the same subject, I am not always truly excited about it. (Don't tell my students.) When I'm feeling a little bored, I put on my best Academy Award act -- I *act* excited about my subject. That excitement is contagious: the students get it from my "act". As a result, I usually catch a good case of excitement from the students. In the end, I may not be excited about my subject, but I am excited (and inspired, really) by the students' new enthusiasm for it. When the class is over, the students tell the administration: "We need more classes with this teacher!"

Lesson #4: The good teacher is well-liked.

Working With The Administration

When I took a draft of this book with me to a convention of school administrators and asked what they felt was missing from the text, each and every one said: "Tell the teachers to follow administrative guidelines." Like what? I asked.

The administration of your school will have policies. Some of these policies are as basic as when class begins and when it ends. ("Is it okay to let my students out early every so often?") Some policies may dictate when you must have your final exams graded and turned in for processing; if you can change student grades; if you should grade on a curve and if so, what curve; if you must give written assignments, quizzes, objective or subjective tests; if you can allow students to have food and drink in the classroom. An important policy question for all teachers is: "what materials will the school pay for?"

Some administrations have many policies; some have only those which arise after you're in trouble. Once you have been hired as a teacher, it's up to you to find out what the policies are and to adhere to them as nearly as possible. If you plan to do something unusual in class, such as the first time you intend to have a guest speaker, you should ask the administration if there is anything special you should know about school policy and your plan.

Most administrative policies are common courtesy and professionalism. Put yourself in the position of the students (or, for that matter, think back to when you were a student). What things did your teachers do that were annoying? The item which comes most readily to mind is not grading papers and quizzes until late in the semester when it is too late to learn from them. When you think about these things, you'll be able to imagine most of your administration's policies.

A long-time friend and post-graduate program administrator complained to me recently that he was going to fire a teacher who had been with him for ten years. What did he do that was so awful? "He just won't get his final grades to me on time," my friend said. "In all of the years he's taught for me, he's never gotten the grades in on time and I've had enough!" It seems a simple enough task: if you are given administrative direction, follow it.

As part of your position as a good teacher:

- Attend orientations and faculty meetings
- Review the faculty handbook
- Review the school catalog
- Create a list of administrators and their area of authority as a quick reference for you and referrals for your students.

Managing the Classroom to Maximize Learning

The Montessori teaching theory has been around for a long time. Montessori subscribes to the belief that children will teach themselves. They are curious. Each student will come to the question and figure out the answer all in his or her time. There are three rules which have as their foundation the belief that people will teach themselves:

- Set fair goals
- Reward achieving the goals
- Reward effort

No-Risk Classroom

To make these rules work, you need to create a "no-risk classroom." This is a place where the teacher does not criticize or make fun of students -- no matter what. Humor is a vital part of teaching, but all humor in the no-risk classroom is "non-combative" humor. The no-risk classroom is a place where every student can speak freely with absolute confidence that he or she will be responded to in the appropriate manner -- with respect, kindness and sincerity.

"No-risk" includes not being at risk from mean-spirited classmates. Any of this behavior must be stopped immediately. Usually a bit of out-of-class counseling does the trick. Once all of your students know that the no-risk classroom works for them if they help make it work for others, they will willingly become part of the no-risk policy.

Set Fair Goals

A fair goal is a clearly-defined, attainable, small step. In other words, a fair goal is not: "win the Nobel Peace Prize." A fair goal is: "read this book before the end of the week." Every new semester should start out with a clear and complete list of these fair goals, small ones and the larger ones which are made up of the small ones. This can be easy for you to create by using the different lessons on your lesson plan.

If your lesson plan says that this week the class will learn about Abraham Lincoln's term as President of the United States, break that large goal into smaller, more easily attainable goals: campaign, election, first year as president, the slave issue, secession, etc. The younger your students, the smaller the break-down of goals should be.

A complete list of fair goals for young children includes what they will be expected to know about each time period: what, who, when, where. For the older children, the list can progress to more complicated concepts: why and how. If, for example, your students will ultimately be responsible for information such as what kinds of weapons were used in the Civil War, your list of goals should include an entry for that: "weapons used." As another example: "Northern Generals" and "Southern Generals." The younger the student, the more information you should fill in.

9.   Weapons used
     a.   breech-loading rifle
     b.   mortars
     c.   rifle-barrel cannons
10. Northern Generals
     a.   Sherman
     b.   Grant
11. Southern Generals
     a.   Lee
     b.   Jackson

If you expect them to know what battles each general fought, include that in your list of goals, as well. If all of the information cannot be found in the text you have chosen, include a list of extra books your students can find at the library and page references for each book. The object of setting fair goals is not "hide the ball."

The younger the student, the more precise goals are required and the more often reinforcement or praise is needed. No matter how old the student is, the student never out-grows the need for fair goals and deserved praise.

Reward achieving goals

Praise in the classroom is primarily teacher-generated. It is catching the student doing something right and acknowledging it: "Correct!" "You are absolutely right!" Questions, as well as answers, deserve praise: "Good question!" "I'm glad you asked that!" If you criticize the students who raise their hands, you teach them not to participate. We teach a mouse to press a lever by giving it a bit of food when it does so. It is a simple learnable response followed by a reinforcing event. If you praise the student who participates, that student will want to participate more. Other students will want that praise, too, so they will try participating.

You can teach the students to praise each other: "John's presentation was excellent, wasn't it?" When you start to applaud, your students will join in. This makes John feel good about his presentation and makes the other students look forward to their own.

You can also teach the students to praise themselves. For the adults: "Take yourself out to dinner tonight" or "Give yourself a pat on the back." For the younger students: "Put a star next to your name!" Self-evaluation and self-esteem are two of the goals of teaching. The world is not a place where people get an abundance of praise from others. Recognizing our own good work and praising ourselves for it is a valuable life-tool.

Reward effort

Praising the student who succeeds is easy. It comes naturally to most people. Rewarding the student who tries but does not succeed does not come so naturally. Rewarding effort has two parts: 1) seeing what is wrong and correcting it; 2) seeing that the student is correcting it and rewarding that. "Well, you didn't complete the assignment, but you did a good job on the first third. Let's agree on a reasonable time period for completing the entire assignment." In-class rewarding effort might be: "Not the answer I was looking for, but good job jumping in with an answer."

Some of this looks like psychological gobbledgook, doesn't it? It did when I first thought about it in the abstract, but when I related the theory to what I actually do in the classroom, I found that it is what makes the students enthusiastic about my class.

I am often asked to "teach" professional responsibility in one 3-hour lecture. It cannot be done. In one 3-hour lecture, however, the students can be made aware of many ethical issues which they will face in the workplace and learn about the tools for finding answers. Those tools include: identifying the problem (something here doesn't look right), categorizing it (this is a conflict of interest), and basic research strategies (start in an encyclopedia, then go to the annotated codes, then to the cases).

These students have never seen me before (so they have no reason to trust me) and they will probably never see me again (so they have no incentive to try hard for me). I want to make my subject interesting and fun, as well as a positive learning experience for the students. I start my talk with a short list of fair goals: "Because I cannot teach you all of the law in three hours, I want to: 1) make you aware of the major ethical issues which you will encounter in the law office (competence issues, fair billing practices, unauthorized practice of law, conflicts of interest, confidentiality); and 2) give you the tools for finding answers."

I always tell the students up-front what will be expected of them after my talk: "there will be a 25 question multiple choice exam," or "because this class is so brief, you will be tested on this material as part of your Introduction to Law class," or whatever the administration has asked me to say. The students want this information. Giving them advance notice about the class goals does not make them listen any harder or not pay attention at all. Often I tell students, "don't write anything: just listen to me because what I am going to tell you makes so much sense, you don't need to write it down in order to remember it." Some students, however, can't listen unless the pens are going, and that's all right, too. The point is to set the goals up front, work methodically through them and let each student learn in his or her own fashion.

Throughout my talk, I use an abundance of energetic praise for the students who ask questions: "Great question!" "I'm glad you asked that!" When the student asks the question which is a lead-in to my next subject, that tells me that the student is tracking with me and is using critical thinking skills to anticipate where I am going.

When I ask a question and get a correct answer, I give praise: "Absolutely right!" I could say: "Okay" as if the answer was the very least I expected, but why not praise the student to make the learning experience more fun for the student and the class? Why not teach that participating is a good thing? Student participation makes your job easier so, ultimately, praising the student will make your teaching more fun.

Let the students teach, too. Teaching is the best way to learn. You can incorporate student-teaching into your classroom by assignment or spontaneously. When you assign a segment of your lesson plan to a student to teach the other students, be prepared on the lesson yourself. No matter what age group you may be teaching, you want your students to get the correct information and your student-teacher may not have it.

Spontaneous student teaching is as easy as: "What a good question! Tell me what you think the answer might be." You can guide the student through to the correct answer in the Socratic method, by asking the smaller, component questions which often have more clear answers, and simultaneously show the student how to arrive at the correct answer him or herself. You are:

- rewarding participation
- teaching critical thinking
- reinforcing self-determination

What to do when you get a "wrong" answer

No honest attempt at participation should be viewed as "wrong." When you ask a question and get an incorrect answer, try saying: "That's not what I was looking for" or "Hang onto that for a minute and I'll get back to you." This type of response is far preferable to "no" or "wrong" or noises indicating that the student has committed an error on a game show. Find another raised hand and another, if necessary, until you find a student with an acceptable answer. If you can't find an acceptable answer within a reasonable number of tries, use the closest "correct" answer and expand on it.

If you have time make an effort to go back to a student with a definitely "wrong" answer and discuss with that student why he or she might have that answer. "Do you see why you were wrong?" is not a good approach if you want that student to participate in the future. The student has already been "wrong" once; you don't want to bring it to everyone's attention again. More often than not, the wrong-answer student has now learned the right answer and will simply say: "Oh yeah. I get it now."

Encourage that student to share the thought process that resulted in an incorrect conclusion. "I liked the answer that Joan gave because it was closer to the answer I was thinking of, but do you want to explain your position?" If the student is comfortable, if the student is secure that yours is a no-risk classroom, the student will share the thought process with you. More often than you think, the student with the seemingly "wrong" answer, was on the right track all along. That student should be praised for the parts of the thought process that were on the right track. This shows other students who might have been using the same erroneous thought process not just that they were wrong but why they were wrong. That's a much more valuable lesson. It shows other students that it is safe to volunteer even when they are not sure of their answer. Giving that student a chance to defend that position and giving praise for it, in addition to teaching self-evaluation, makes you look like the sincere, respectful, kind and fair teacher that you are!

Some answers are so close to being correct that it is not worth "correcting" them. Deciding which questions can take "close" answers, which need to be "correct", and which can more easily be "corrected" will ultimately be your decision. You must balance the importance of that particular answer, its proximity to the exact answer you were looking for, and the strengths and needs of the individual student who provided the answer. This is an equation which has none of its own rules. You can only use the other rules which apply to the good teacher: be polite, respectful, sincere, kind, cheerful and fair.

Depending upon the pace of the class, a wrong answer may simply get a big smile from me and a high-energy: "Good try, but not what I wanted," before I move on to the next student. I'm balancing not hurting the student with a "wrong" answer with getting the right answer to the class quickly. Part of the balance is the way you say it, and not necessarily the words you use. You tell the class with your voice, facial expressions and body language that you are happy that the student is trying. This is part of rewarding effort. You want to get the right answer to the class but sometimes you won't have a lot of time to "rehabilitate" the wrong-answer student.

Lesson #5: The good teacher sets fair goals, praises progress and rewards the students who try.

When There is No Right or Wrong

Many classes you will teach have no right or wrong answers at all.   In these classes, creative and thoughtful debate, logical argument, and articulate expression all deserve praise. I will never forget the English literature class I took in college. I was an English major. The next class in the order set out for me by my counselor was a class in poetry. To my dismay, the teacher insisted that we learn his interpretation of every poem and subscribe to his theories of the significance of each word. I changed my major to Political Science.

Lesson #6: The good teacher gives the student an opportunity to express views and defend positions.

Shake off the Day

If you will be teaching at night, you will have to deal with the problems of the day before you go into the classroom. It is manifestly unfair to make your students pay for something that someone did to you in your workplace earlier in the day. When you are stressed, take a minute outside the door and tell yourself exactly that. "Why am I teaching? It's certainly not for the money. It must be because I enjoy it. If I'm going to enjoy it, I'll set my other problems aside right now and enjoy this class. I'll come back to the other problems after class."

As an extreme example of why I teach, I can tell you about an experience I had many years ago. I had hurt my back lifting something. I had been in constant pain for a few days. Although I was grumpy and unpleasant, I went to class anyway. I started out painfully stiff, but I began to teach and to concentrate on the lesson and the students. It was a good class and after the class was over I realized that my back was fine! I had no pain then, and it never came back (until the next time I wrenched something). I teach because I love to teach. Why are you teaching?

Shake off Your Teachers

If you are a lawyer, shake off your memories of law school. You do not have to teach in the monotonous and degrading method to which you may have been subjected in school. If you are a doctor, put aside the teacher who stared at the light fixtures and talked to hear his or her own voice. Think about a teacher you had in college or graduate school whom you thought was a good teacher. What was it about that teacher that you liked? That well-liked teacher had energy, made the class fun, interacted with the students, had a sense of humor, listened to the students, was prepared and organized and therefore self-confident. Now try to be like that teacher.

I had a teacher for an 8:00 a.m. class my first year in law school who was so interesting that I actually made it to class (almost) every morning. When I started to teach, I called him on the telephone and said, "I want to be a teacher just like you. How do you do it?" He said simply: "It's fun. I like to do it." On the other hand, I had some of those traditional, grumpy, inflexible, and rude professors. Make note of them and pledge not to be like them. Some of the things you may have hated as a student become your guides for being a better teacher.

The First Class

At the very beginning of the semester, you should introduce yourself to the class and set the ground rules. If you are teaching adults, you want to give your name and a telephone number where you can be reached outside of class, either a school office telephone number or another phone number. If you are teaching children, you want to write these things down and instruct the children to take the hand-out to their parents. You should give the students a <u>brief</u> autobiography. Take a few minutes to tell them those things about yourself which make you qualified to teach this course: education, training, work experience, similar courses you have taught, books you have written and other credits. Do not give the class your life history.

Ground rules should include items such as eating and drinking in class. ("I allow drinking until someone spills. I do not allow eating because students should be participating, not chewing.") You should hand out your class syllabus and reading list so the students know what is expected of them in advance of each class. You should tell them when exams will be, what kind of exams (what will be the method of testing) and any special rules about the exams: open book, timed, take-home, that you do or do not review and re-grade exams. (See Grading the Exam, page 78)

Other considerations for the first class are policies concerning:

• what the students should call you
• books and materials the students will need
• absenteeism
• tardiness
• how role will be taken
• seating chart
• raising hand for questions or not
• breaks
• classes to be canceled and make-up classes
• holidays
• field trip dates
• guest speaker dates
• late assignments
• format and timing of exams
• how the course will be graded
• policies about re-reading exams
• policies about make-up exams

Many of these ground rules apply to teachers of very young students, as well. Although the students might not have much of an appreciation for some of the rules, the students' parents will: no gum in class; no personal toys which are not for sharing; no soda for "milk time."

The ground rules you set during your first class should not change. Course objectives and grading criteria should not change. Exceptions should be avoided. They cause confusion in the younger students and resentment in the older.

An introduction to the no-risk classroom is an essential part of the first class, as well.

It is important to convey your self-confidence in the first class. You are prepared so you can speak comfortably and use your natural sense of humor, as opposed to a speech with memorized jokes. You are cheerful and happy to be teaching this class to these students.

Lesson #7: The good teacher is prepared for the first class and every class thereafter.

Teaching Materials

Ordinarily a textbook will be your primary teaching tool. Students should be given clear instructions regarding what should be read and when (i.e. reading assignments should be completed before the class during which we will be discussing the material). In addition to the text, a workbook of additional hypotheticals, short answer, multiple choice and true/false questions is an excellent idea for the students' self-testing. Some textbooks include these self-testing tools.

The textbook must be at the appropriate learning level for your students. Studies indicate that students with a reading level two grades below that of the text have only a 5% chance of earning a passing grade.

Only ask the students to buy a book which you actually intend to use. It is a good policy to ensure that there is a copy of the text on reserve in the library for the student who cannot afford to buy the book.

Although the Supreme Court has said that much copyright protection is lifted for teaching purposes, photocopying large portions or chapters of someone else's work is not advisable for a number of reasons: 1) the student should not have to work from photocopied material; 2) the author should be given the benefit of his or her work by way of royalties; 3) the publisher should be given the benefit of its work by way of purchase price.

When choosing teaching materials, consider the cost to the student, if any. You should know, or find out from the publisher, what the suggested retail price of each assigned book is. If your school bookstore is selling the book for more than that and the cost creates a hardship for your students, you can discuss that with the appropriate authority: the bookstore manager or your school dean. Bookstores are given a discount by the publisher so that the bookstore can make a profit when the book is sold at the suggested retail price. If your bookstore is pricing the book at substantially more than the suggested retail, you may want to contact the publisher directly. If the book is too expensive, let the publisher know.

As the teacher, you should be aware of the expense of any item which is necessary for class. A bar of soap for art & crafts is not very expensive and most students will be able to come up with one; however, you are the polite, kind and fair person in charge and if there are students who cannot afford whatever it is, either provide the materials through the school or by yourself, or change the project so that no one is left out.

If you are a professional such as a lawyer, doctor or accountant, you should not use or distribute copies of your files or other documents belonging to your clients. The secrets of your clients or patients are secrets even after the matter or case is concluded, even after the pleadings are public record. In other words, that something is on file at the courthouse does not mean that your students would have known about it if you had not told them. Yes, we teach by using our experiences. However, extreme caution should be taken to not give the students a reason to believe you cannot be trusted with their confidences by giving them other people's confidential information.

Listen to the Students

Sometimes I catch myself asking a question in class and then not really listening to the answer I get. I just say the answer I wanted (my "right" answer) as if I am repeating what the student said, and I move on to the next point. Usually this happens when I am rushed. When I catch myself doing this, I stop and apologize to that student. No lesson plan is so important that the good teacher doesn't have time to listen.

Students will often be the ones to tell you the things you need to know: ("Did you know that tomorrow is a school holiday?" is one of my favorites.) Students will more often tell you things they need to say to someone. They need things from teachers which have little to do with education. Listening to the students will help you recognize these things.

We all learn differently. When you listen to the students, you will hear what they need and how they need to learn. Some people think in visual images while others excel in abstract, logical reasoning. When the student speaks to you with images, it is a safe bet that the student needs to get images back from you. All of our students are "smart" in their own ways. The good teacher listens to the students to hear how each student can excel.

Students will also tell you things about your teaching. If your administration does not already conduct an evaluation or review at the end of the semester or school year, you might consider doing it. If your review is anonymous, you will probably get more honest answers. You can ask the students what they thought about the text, the guest speaker, the classroom setting and your teaching skills. When reviewing the responses, don't take everything to heart, but look for common themes. If everyone in the class thought the text was too difficult, well, maybe it was.

Lesson #8: The good teacher listens to the students.

The Logical Lesson Plan

You should know where you are going before you begin your journey with a classroom full of students. If this is the first time you are going to teach this particular class, try to get a lesson plan from the former teacher or from the administration. If there is no lesson plan available, ask the administration for an outline of what they expect you to teach. If a book was used in this class before, and the book is a good one, you can take your lesson plan right out of the table of contents. If you plan to use different books, or magazines, or articles from other sources, or even movies, the task of making a coherent lesson plan must begin with your thoughts on what you want the students to know at the end of the class. Once you have your main goal in mind, backtrack from there to see what smaller goals you need to set to get to that main goal.

A lesson plan is extremely important for the good teacher. Your students need to be secure in the knowledge that you have a plan for them, that you are not just flopping aimlessly about. Giving the students your lesson plan on the first day of class gives them a sense that you are prepared and knowledgeable, that you will be a good teacher. It also forces you to know ahead of time what you will be teaching and in what order. Planning all of your lessons in advance of the first class will also force you to give thought to alternative teaching methods such as movies, research projects, class field trips and the like.

Your administration should be able to provide some sample lessons plans for your assistance in compiling your own lesson plan. Each week's plan should tell the students (and the teacher) what is expected of them, what goals have been set. It also gives them an outline for studying for exams.

A good lesson plan not only includes your class plans, but any school-wide activities. Your lesson plan must also account for school holidays and conflicts in your own schedule. One way to keep track of all these dates is to photocopy a calendar and keep it in your three-ring binder (see pg. 4). It may be best to write on the calendar in pencil. Some good teachers give the students these calendars to help get them organized and prepared for each class.

Lesson plans should be mandatory, but they are not. If there is no existing lesson plan for your class from which you can work, you will have to invent the wheel. When you leave your class, consider leaving a copy of your lesson plan behind as a courtesy to the next teacher.

The "Invisible Line"

Administrators talk about crossing the invisible line as the fastest way to lose control of your classroom. Crossing the line includes: telling risqué jokes, using obscenities, chumming around with the students, criticizing the administration, and agreeing that Professor So-and-So is a lousy teacher.

A teacher I know well taught the Thursday evening 7:00 - 10:00 class. Because it was a class held late at night and late in the week, she had trouble keeping the students awake. As a result, she developed a habit of interjecting obscenities, very loud obscenities, into her usual lecture. It kept the students awake and she thought it was a useful teaching tool. The problem was that she had trouble taking those obscenities out of her every-day speech after having so successfully used them the night before. When swearing turned into a habit, she was admonished by not one but a number of administrators. She had crossed the line.

Some administrators will tell you that "Professor Jones" is the appropriate way for the students to address you. In some schools the teacher's first name is used. New teachers may find that the use of a title (Mr. ___; Ms. ___; Professor ___) will help them create the level of respect they need for a successful class. Without some direction from your administration, it is a personal choice. The students need to take their direction from you. Like the other things you will tell your students on the first day, instructing the class on the proper way to address you creates an important first impression.

Students will invariably ask for something you don't have. The easiest way to respond is to blame whatever it is on the administration: "I wanted to show you a video today, but the school wouldn't spring for it." This approach is also the easiest way to not be invited back to teach at the conclusion of your contract. You and the administration should always appear to be a united front. Do not burden the students with the problems you may have with the administration or other teachers.

Do not invite your students into your private life. Do not share your secrets with them. Be sincere, but keep your distance.

Conducting Classes

Getting the Information Across

Extemporaneous speaking is the most widely used method of teaching. You speak from an outline to stay organized, but because you haven't tried to memorize every word and because you are not reading something prepared earlier, you express yourself in a natural conversational manner. It is easy to look at your students and keep their attention. It also gives you the flexibility to add or omit details based on audience reaction and interest.

The average person will not listen to lecturing for more than 20 minutes. Every subject can lend itself to discussion so you shouldn't need to talk non-stop for 20 minutes. Students learn more when they are part of the question, so give the class a hypothetical and get them to discuss the answer: What do you think would have happened if President Lincoln had desegregated the army during the civil war? Because it is a hypothetical, there are no concrete answers. Everyone will have an opinion. Perhaps an interesting debate will spontaneously erupt in class. The trick is to make the subject real to the students, to get them personally involved, to make the discussion important to them.

You are still in charge of managing the discussion, however. You are not giving up control of the classroom. You can start with two students debating opposing points of view and allow other students to interject their points of view by raising their hands. If you allow everyone to speak whenever they want, you will have a free-for-all shouting match. On the other hand, sometimes those free-for-alls are just what it takes to get the students excited about your subject.

Technology has provided some alternatives to "just lecturing," as well. Computers, computerized projections, overhead projectors, digital image projectors and educational videos are just a few examples of different teaching methods which can enhance your classroom presentation by getting the information across in a new and interesting way. Some of this equipment is expensive and may not be available to you. Almost every school has access to an overhead projector, however. Overhead panels are as easy to make as sending a transparency (available at office supply stores) through a photocopier or your computer's printer. If you don't have access to that equipment, you can draw on transparencies with felt tip pens. Simple and inexpensive, overhead transparencies are a terrific way for even the non-technical teacher to display everything from the class outline to illustrative cartoons.

Dealing with Questions: Deflect for Learning

From the beginning of the class, you should be clear with the students regarding how you will accept questions. Some people prefer to wait until the end of the class period. I don't recommend that because many questions are so context-based that they don't make sense later. On the other hand, you don't want to be distracted by a question in the middle of a thought and you don't want some poor student to spend five minutes with a hand in the air. Try acknowledging the hand: "I see your hand, hold on to your question for a minute." Then the student can sit in a more comfortable position. When you are finished with your thought or section of material, you can go back to that student. This requires, of course, that you can remember the students with questions in the right order.

Questions are good. They bring the students into the presentation of information. They make you think. They make the students think. Encourage questions but remind the students that there is rarely only one "correct" answer. When a question is asked, then, it is good to get some different points of view for the answer. This is "deflecting" the question. The question is asked of you, but you deflect it by asking others what their views are.

Many questions begin with: "Would it be okay to..."

The hypo: "I see a clerk steal money out of your
            wallet."
The question: "What is my responsibility?"
First answer: "I will confront the person."

The next student asks: "Would it be okay to tell the
office manager instead?"   *Deflect* that question.
Because students learn more when they are part of
the learning experience, turn to another student
and ask: "What do you think?" or simply bounce
the question back to the student who asked it. Your
personal answer, your limits or beliefs, are not the
lessons you were hired to teach. You were hired to
make the students aware of the questions and give
them the tools to find their own solutions.

Whether you choose to answer the question or to
deflect it, remember to be polite and treat the
student with respect. One of the most horrible
learning experiences I ever had was this response to
a question: "If you were a man, you wouldn't have
asked such a stupid question." Never belittle a
student for asking a question. When you do, you
teach all of the students not to ask questions. A
handy quote for the students: "The only 'stupid'
question is the one which went un-asked."

When You Don't Know the Answer

As many years as I have been studying and teaching ethics, I don't know all of the answers. The best response to the question, then, is: "I don't know." Students appreciate this honesty much more than they will appreciate your obvious attempt to fake an answer. In the classroom, a good response to the question you can't answer is: "I don't know. Why don't you look up the answer for us and report back next class meeting?" That "empowers" the student and gets you off the hook. If you send the student off to research the question do not rely on the student for the correct or complete answer. Look up the answer yourself. During the next class meeting, let the student report and then add whatever else you think the class should know.

The alternatives to admitting that you do not know the answer to a question are: faking an answer or giving bad information. As to the former -- the students will know. The latter isn't a great choice either.

When You Make a Mistake

My fifth grade teacher told my class that if we could look through the eye of the common housefly it would be like looking through a screen door. I don't know why I knew that his statement was incorrect, but I did, and I corrected him. To this day, I remember him red-faced, stubbornly insisting that his statement was correct and mine (that it would be like looking at thousands of the same image) was not and I was a stupid little girl for trying to correct HIM, the TEACHER. This image flashes through my mind whenever I make a mistake in class. I say: "You're right. Good catch! Thanks for making sure the rest of the class got it straight."

Sometimes I am talking so fast and trying to get so much information across that my mind is going faster than my tongue. I make a mistake. Sometimes I am just out-and-out wrong because I have misread something or gotten bad information from somewhere or reached the wrong conclusion all by myself. I err. You do, too.

It's okay. Acknowledge it, correct it, and move on. The students will respect you for it.

Lesson #9: The good teacher is honest.

How to Ask a Question

The good teacher gets the students involved in the learning process. To do that, the teacher needs to get the students to participate. The students will only participate if the rewards of participating are greater than the risks. As a result, the best class is a no-risk class. Positive feedback is key.   Three important components of this are: 1) asking a question that more than one student can answer; 2) asking a question that they *can* answer; and 3) being willing to accept something other than one particular answer.[3]

A "yes-or-no" answer question invites failure. "Was the breech-loading rifle used by the Confederate Army during the Civil War?" Only a maximum of two students can answer this question and there is a substantial risk that the first student to answer will have the wrong answer. Instead, ask a broader question which invites many students to participate in a no-risk environment.

"What can you tell me about the breech-loading rifle?"

One student will say that it's a type of "gun," and another student will say it's "a rifle that they used

---

[3] Sometimes this is not possible. Two plus three will always equal five and no other answer is acceptable. The solution is to ask the students questions which challenge them, not scare them away from participating.

in the Civil War." Be enthusiastic for these students. "Good!" What else?" This invites more. It invites discussion. It allows each student to answer at his or her own level of understanding. Many answers are correct. Everyone wins.

There is no difference in approach for adult students. "In the reading, the author discusses five factors. What are they?" This question will probably draw seven, eight or more "factors." You can prioritize them by listing them on the blackboard, not in the order they are stated, but in the order of importance for your lesson. If one "factor" suggested by a student is a sub-set of another "factor", tell the student "Good! That's a part of this one" and list it accordingly. In this fashion, all of your volunteers are "correct" and you can give the class the "most correct" five factors while never telling a student "no, you're wrong."

The goal is to give the students the feeling of success. When they are successful in your class, they will strive to be more successful in other classes. Many students who start out neglecting reading assignments "see the light" because of this feeling of success and become well-prepared and good participants.

Call the Students By Name

When you enter the classroom for the first time, make an effort to learn a few students' names. Some will be easy. Mr. Henderson looks just like a Henderson you knew years ago. Ms. Treeple is tall like a tree. Ms. Smith is, well, Ms. Smith. Make an effort to learn a few new names every class period. The students who sit in the front will be easy. They are anxious to be known and remembered (assuming that they are in the front by choice). The students in the back will be harder. They do not want to be known. If you have a perverse sense of humor, you might begin by learning the "back row" students first and see if they move forward. Many students will be pleased that you have made the effort.

One way to learn student names is a seating chart. If this idea works for you, you should start on the first day of class and instruct the students not to change seats. You might try prop-up signs (or name tags) for student names. Have each student put his or her prop-up sign at the front of his or her desk. Again, many students will think its nice that you have made an effort, even if you are bad with names. You might even explain it that way: "I want to learn your names and I'm not good at it so these signs will help." If you want to get a laugh, add: "Those of you who don't want me to know you can give the signs back to me." The smart students will immediately know that any signs you

get back will be names you will definitely
remember! Take the signs with you at the end of
each class. The students think it's funny to mix up
the signs. Alternatively, they will lose them.

After a few semesters, you'll find it becomes much
easier to remember names. When I guest lecture, I
call on every student and say first: "Tell me your
name." The student says: "Judy." I say: "Okay,
Judy. What's your question?" (or: "what's your
answer?") I learn each name by repeating it
(sometimes several times) while talking to that
student. By the end of a three hour lecture, I know
everyone in the room. Some of my friends call this
a "parlor trick". I call it part of being a good teacher.

Call on Everyone

Some students want to participate. Some students do not. Avoid the temptation to call on the same "volunteer" students all the time. As you get to know your students better, you will learn what "level" of question each student can answer. When you have an easier question, try calling on the student who will be challenged by it, not the student who knows the answer. Remember to ask the question in an open fashion to give the student room to be right. The job you have been hired to do includes teaching all of the students, not just the ones who volunteer, and not just the ones who are at the top of the class. Of course, you don't want to embarrass students by continually asking them questions they cannot answer.

As our classrooms become increasingly diverse, we see more names which seem difficult to pronounce. The more you try to get these names right, the more the students will appreciate your honesty and sincerity. When you find yourself not calling on a student out of fear of mispronouncing his or her name, work with the student (perhaps there's a nickname which the student prefers) and practice pronunciation outside of the classroom. If you appear sincere in your desire to learn all of the names, the students will reward you by forgiving your poor pronunciation.

To be sure that you call on all of the students, you may want to make a notation on your roll sheet or seating chart each time you call on each student during the semester. This will also serve you at the end of the semester when you want to give certain students extra "participation points" in accordance with your administration's policies.

The goal of the good teacher is to have students participate because they want to. All of the lessons in this book will help to make you a good teacher. Students will work harder, be more forgiving, and participate more for a good teacher.

Body Language

Get out from behind that lectern! Waive your arms! Gesticulate! Point to students when you call on them. (See above: Call the Students By Name) Look them in the face. You probably don't know everything you want to say by heart, but there are many times (such as when you are involving students in discussions among themselves) when you won't need your notes. Take those opportunities to walk around. Make the students turn their heads to see you. It's a good way to see if they're awake. Nothing is more boring than something that is standing still, except maybe something that is pacing in a monotonous fashion.

Write the crucial points of your lecture on the blackboard or put them on the overhead projector. A recent study showed that, on average, students record about 90% of the information written on a blackboard. Additionally, this provides a handy enlarged lecture outline for you. Now you can walk around the classroom and refer to your "notes" when you need them. Because it serves as an outline for the class, the students love it. When there is no blackboard or overhead, put your outline on 3 x 5 index cards and keep the cards in your pocket for reference so you are not tied to the podium.

Use body language to encourage and praise the students. When I want more people to volunteer, I make an exaggerated beckoning motion with my hands which says, "Come on! Give it a try!" When I have a lot of energy sparking in class and everyone is excited about learning, I make the "OK" sign with my fingers and wave my arms around for everyone to see. You won't look silly if you use this extreme form of body language. You'll look like a person who is having fun teaching. Motion your students to come with you into your enthusiasm for your subject and watch how much easier and more fun your class becomes.

Take a look at your posture. Do you slump unnaturally? Try straightening up. Throw your shoulders back. Wave your arms. Smile. Look like you're proud of what you do. You're in control; you're self-confident; you're a good teacher. Congratulations!

Think Creatively About New Ways to Teach

One of the problems you will no doubt face is that your students think that whatever subject you are teaching (from accounting to zoology) is boring. You can dispel this misconception immediately by making the students part of the learning experience, by bringing their experiences into the classroom, by using the classroom management techniques of fair goals and rewards. When your students learn that your subject is interesting, they will want to participate (presuming you reward them for it) and they will make the subject even more interesting for themselves.

Nonetheless, there are more and less interesting ways to present even an interesting subject. Lecture is probably the most boring because it is the least interactive. The use of hypotheticals is not boring for the students involved in the discussion but may be for those who are watching.

There are some very interesting practical assignments, experiments, models (good for teaching battles!), field trips, research assignments, videos, films, slides shows, guest speakers and other teaching tools available to you. Try small group discussions and letting your students teach. Interactive learning is available to you on a computer or in-person.

Do not let "boring" become a self-fulfilling prophesy. Some of the attitudes which will keep you in the "boring teacher" department are: 1) I tried it once and it didn't work; 2) the administration won't let me; and 3) we don't have the money. There are ways to beat those prophesies. For example, if you tried a guest speaker once and the students didn't get anything out of it, perhaps you simply chose the wrong speaker. Analyze what went wrong and fix it. Try again. If your school does not have the money to pay for the video, call the publisher. Maybe they have a rental policy or an educational discount. If you don't want to take the money out of your pocket to rent a video, ask the class. Most likely, one of your students has access to the video you would like to show to the class. You can also tape movies or documentaries off of your television set for purposes of teaching. If you're in doubt about the propriety, call the copyright owner and ask.

If your students do not have money for extra books or other teaching materials, contact the publisher or manufacturer. Often, there are slightly damaged books or whathaveyou available at practically no cost. Get creative.

Try having the students act out scenarios. When teaching students how to be lawyers, paralegals, architects, billing clerks or any other person who will ever have to communicate with another person as part of the job, try having them act out that communication in different fact patterns: the customer is angry; the customer is disappointed; the customer will not be appeased. Life is filled with an endless list of creative ways of teaching "real life" situations to students.

There is a story about a teacher in a poor urban area who wanted his students to go to a museum. The students protested that they did not have the money to pay for admission. After arranging it with the museum, the teacher "plotted" with his students to sneak into the museum. Because they thought they were involved in a break-in, all of the students attended and enjoyed the museum once they got inside. It was a creative solution to a common problem. Try creativity, not defeatism.

Lesson #10: The good teacher is creative.

The Substance of Your Class

Core subjects

You should decide before you begin teaching, sometime when you are creating your lesson plan, which are the most important topics in your subject. For example, most experts would agree that the "core" subjects in professional responsibility are: unauthorized practice of law, confidentiality, conflicts of interest, and competence issues including client funds and ethical fees. When my professional responsibility course is 3 or 4 hours long, I can cover those four subjects. They are the subjects which will most likely present actual ethical problems for my students when they go into the workplace.

No matter what subject you are teaching, you want to be sure to cover the "core" topics. If your class is preempted by something, you can quickly and easily focus the students on the core topics and forego the remainder. The point is that, having decided in advance what four or five topics are the most important, you will be prepared for any eventuality.

Recapping

If you are teaching a sequential class, one where the topic you covered during the last class session is connected to the topic you will cover in this class session, you should consider spending a few minutes "recapping" the core points of the last class or the last few classes. If you write your class outline on the board and highlight the part you will be covering during this class session, you will help the students put what they are learning into the "big picture" perspective. Recapping helps to keep the students aware of the big goals and starting out each class with a short list of what you will be covering in this class helps get the students focused on the smaller goals.

Teaching from a text

When you are choosing a text for your class, choose one which allows you to easily divide the book into reading assignments. For example, *Ethics for the Legal Assistant, Third Edition* was written to fit into a 12 hour semester. (One hour each week for 12 weeks.) My lesson plans require the students to read a chapter each week and take a midterm and final exam. Of course, if your course is longer or shorter than the text planned for, or if you are using one text as a supplement to another, you have to adjust your lesson plans.

There are many textbooks available now in every subject. Unless your administration tells you otherwise, don't think that you have to use the same book your predecessor used. Go to the library or contact the publishers (they will often have a salesperson call on you) and find the text that will suit you, your lesson plans, and your students.

Practical assignments

Most "book learnin'" means little until it is put into practice. For that reason, incorporate practical assignments into your lesson plan. A practical assignment is an out of class assignment which has as its goal getting the students to take something they have learned in class and put it into practice in their own life. This teaches critical thinking. Because I think that the practical aspect of education is so important, I teach my students how to research each subject and recognize how the subject comes up in real life. That way, when the time comes, the students will be able to spot and characterize issues, and back up their understanding of the facts, or satisfy their curiosity, with research.

For example, my story about the eye of the common housefly (pg. 38) can have a practical application for almost every age group. The young student may be asked to catch some flies and watch them or draw a picture of what it would be like to look out of a fly's eye. An older student may be asked to research how houseflies carry diseases and report back to the class with a paper on the subject. A college student could write an entire term paper on the common housefly.

No matter what age group, once the student is aware of books and other resources on the subject for his or her age group, when the student is curious about the housefly, he or she can go to the library (or access the Internet!) and research the charming little fellow. Most importantly, because your students are not bogged down with the "I don't know where to start" problem, they are more likely to learn on their own.

It's very exciting when students take initiative because of something you've taught them to do. You're teaching self-direction and self-determination.

Remember Lesson #2: the good teacher shows the student how to learn.

As you become more familiar with your subject matter, you'll think of your own practical assignments, field trips, movies, computer programs, internet sites, and extra research materials to enhance your class. Don't think that you need to integrate everything into your first teaching assignment. Experiment on your own before trying something new in class.

Quick List of Hints for Successful Classes

1. deflect questions: students learn from them

2. admit mistakes and make them a learning tool

3. ask questions that invite answers

4. learn students' names by seating charts or tags

5. call on all of your students

6. structure a question the student can answer

7. use body language

8. use creative teaching techniques

9. concentrate on core topics

10. recap earlier class lessons

11. use practical assignments

The Students You Will Meet

How to Relate to the Disgruntled Student

You will hear experienced teachers say "there's one in every class." In any class you will teach for any length of time there will be a disgruntled, bad-tempered student. The student is mad at the administration, or at you, or at life in general. The student is a loud-mouth. The student is disrespectful. Each day before class, you pray that this student will be absent. Take heart. There is a way to deal with this student.

The Angry Student
Talk to the angry student privately to try to discover the cause of the negative attitudes and help the student focus on the cause. If the student is angry with the administration, for instance, discuss ways for him to voice his anger to the administration and encourage him to have a positive attitude in your classroom. If the student is mad at you, let the student vocalize the anger ("You gave me a bad grade and I didn't deserve it!") and talk about ways to correct the problem ("You didn't get the grade you thought you deserved. What can I do to help you do better on the next exam?" If you prefer: "I'll review the exam again. Maybe you're right.") If the student is just basically a pain-in-the-neck type of angry person, discuss ways to focus the anger outside of the classroom.

The Loud-Mouth Student

Recently, I was giving a guest lecture in a school in a distant state. The loud mouth was in fine form that evening and was wise-cracking at my every pause. I called a coffee break and approached Mr. Loud-Mouth at his desk after the other students had left the room. I said, "I understand that you are probably way ahead of the rest of these students in this subject. You have obviously taken an interest and studied it previously. However, the school asked me to teach this class this evening. I would appreciate it if you would let me earn my pay for the students who do not know as much as you do." He didn't make another crack for the rest of the evening. In fact, his contributions were so positive for the rest of the evening that the teacher later asked me if I had bribed him.

If your loud-mouth is trying to control your class, try delivering your class instruction from that student's shoulder. Stand next to or directly behind the loud-mouth and get in his or her "space." Few students will raise their hands or interrupt class when the teacher is standing right next to them. Your presence in Loud-Mouth's space sends a message: the teacher is in control of this class.

If you have a "what if...." type of loud-mouth, it may help to set a limit. "Tonight we have a lot of material to cover so I'll allow you two 'what-if' questions." You can also try: "You need to hold those extra hypotheticals for after class."

The Angry Mob

I had one entire class of students who were angry at the administration of the school. They felt that the school had promised them things which were not delivered. Every night, instead of talking about the subject I was teaching, the students wanted to talk about how angry they were. (Unfortunately or not, ethics class is always perceived as a good place to discuss anger with the school, the other teachers and whatever else.) Finally, I told them: "I was hired to teach ethics here and I would like to do that. I have problems, too. I get angry, just like you do, but I do not bring it into the classroom and make you listen to it. I shake off the rest of my day before I enter the classroom and deal with the people who make me angry on their time, not yours. That's what we're going to do in this class. If you have a problem with the administration, make an appointment to see the Dean and take up those problems with her. Before you walk into this classroom, put those other issues aside and be ready to talk about our topic." That speech does not always work right away, but it undoubtedly soaks in by the third recital.

Don't buy into the anger. "Do you think I'm a fool?" is just an invitation to the disgruntled student to make your classroom life hell. "If you think you know everything, why don't you come up here and teach the whole class" will get you a smart-mouth at the front of the classroom. You are no longer in control. Your classroom is a mess.

Stay calm and remember Lesson #1. Repeat it to yourself. Put a smile on your face, discipline the smart-mouth in accordance with the school's policies and, if all else fails, <u>act</u> like you're in control until you are.

No one speech will be right for all disgruntled student problems but here are the common threads:

- Do not make a personal attack on the disgruntled student.
- Try to focus the student on the real target of the problem.
- Use questions, not statements or demands. Perhaps the student just needs to talk.
- Offer suggestions for dealing with the real target.
- Encourage the student to have a positive attitude in your classroom.
- Invite the student to not attend class if the student cannot attend with a positive attitude.
- Discipline the student as necessary in accordance with school policies.
- Most importantly, Lesson #1: be polite, respectful, sincere, kind, as cheerful as possible under the circumstances, and fair. This is not an adversarial proceeding.

How to Deal With the Hostile Question

The watch-words for the teacher when the student has an angry or hostile question are: delay, depersonalize, and deflect.

Everyone in the room will recognize the hostile questioner. This student has some agenda which is probably not in the best interests of the rest of the class. This student is trying to take control of your class, or is seeking revenge for something (real or imagined) you (or the school administration) have done. More commonly, this student is merely trying to get attention. Whatever the reason, you want to handle the hostile questioner in a manner which serves your goals for the class.

Delay by repeating the substance of the question, using the part of the question which relates to the subject which you were discussing in class. *Depersonalize* the hostility by rephrasing the question in a less hostile manner. Use this rephrasing to draw the attention of the class away from the hostile questioner and toward you and your mastery of the subject. Then *deflect* the question, or parts of the question if it is multi-faceted, back to the hostile student to answer his or her own question, or to other members of the class for their input.

The good teacher can respond to the hostile question in a fashion that maintains control of the classroom and shows the questioner that whatever his or her goal, it will not be achieved by the use of a hostile attitude. By using the goals-praise methods described in this book, you can get the student the desired attention in a positive fashion which will enhance this student's learning experience and the other students', as well.

Mind you, no one can say this is easy. It can be done and, done correctly, keeps you in complete control of your class as a self-confident teacher. It enhances the students' respect for you as the well-liked teacher. The exhilaration you will experience each time you "win over" a hostile questioner will make all of your effort worthwhile.

As with all other student-problem situations (as well as, by the way, administrative-problem situations), Lesson #1 will put you in the best position for a favorable resolution.

How to Motivate the Poorly-Motivated Student

Whether you are teaching at a university, community college, vocational school, or traditional K-12, you will have a student who is not motivated. Perhaps this student is being forced to attend school; perhaps this student just doesn't want to take your class. In general, this student is a drag on the class. The normal reaction is to ignore this student and focus on the people who want to be there. I encourage you, however, to make an effort to motivate poorly-motivated students for their own sake. Sometimes, making the poorly-motivated student "special" will be all the motivation that's needed.

Special interests
    Relate your classroom topic to one which interests the poorly-motivated student. When learning becomes fun, the apathy is dispelled.

Special praise
    Don't over-challenge this student, but encourage him or her to keep up. Give extra praise for participating. Pay attention to the kind of praise to which this student responds.

Special projects
    Try offering a special project to pique his or her interest. Don't let the poorly motivated students slow the class, but try not to abandon them.

How to Assist the Poorly-Prepared Student

You will inevitably get a student who is not prepared for the subject you are teaching or the level at which you are teaching. Perhaps this student had a poor elementary school education so his or her reading skills are not up to par. Whatever this student's reasons for being poorly-prepared, you were hired to teach this student. In some cases that may mean many extra hours bringing the student up to the level of the other students. Social promotions are "out." Preparedness and learning is "in." If you have a student who is the result of social promotions, it is up to you and every other teacher to bring this student up to speed.

I have worked with students in post graduate programs who have poor study habits. There are a number of good books in your library which can assist these students. The lazy student or the student who does not want to be helped probably will not be helped. The student who can be made to recognize his or her deficiencies and who wants to correct them should be given all of the encouragement you can muster including references to books, videos and audio tapes on studying, relating personal experiences which assisted you in studying (even if you have to embellish them!) and spending extra time with the student to encourage and ratify new habits.

When you have a student whose problems are more severe such as a reading disability, you may want to seek advice from your administration. If they are aware of the problem and instruct you to "do what you can and pass him along to the next class," you should take some time to think about that. This view, though popular in the past, is not the best thing for this student.

Solutions? You can ask the school for counseling for this student to get the assistance needed to improve those basic skills. Personally assisting the student is an option. Certainly encouraging the student to get the basic skills needed to accomplish the goals of your class is something we all have the time to do. You might do the research and give this student some telephone numbers of places where assistance is available. Passing the student on to the next teacher is not an option.

Know When It Is Time to Get Help From the Administration

As a teacher it is easy to forget that you do not work alone. You may be the highest authority in the classroom, but the school administration is there to help you and your students. Recognize your limits in dealing with and helping students. When your limits are exceeded, or you think they may be in the near future, get help.

I have a teacher friend who tells me this lesson: "When the students come to me for help the first time, I tell them the way; when they come the second time, I show them the way; when they come back the third time, I send them away." This is meant as a joke, of course. Sending the student away isn't the answer, but getting assistance from the administration can be the right answer to many problems. When you can't handle a problem, or you don't know how the school would like the problem handled, get help.

How to Deal With Different Learning Levels

When I first started teaching paralegals, I taught as I had been taught in law school. I had an exceptionally bright group of students that semester and they kept up with me. They never complained and, as they did not know what to expect from paralegal school, they thought that I was teaching correctly. It struck me when I was grading their essays, however, that my level of teaching was inappropriate for several reasons: 1) I had not taken the students' prior education into consideration; 2) I had not taken the goal of paralegal education into consideration so I had focused on legal theory instead of the practical aspects of law; 3) I had not listened to the level of the students' questions; 4) I had not tested the students' progress, I had tested instead the level which I wanted them to have achieved; 5) I had not considered the extraordinary effort the students had put in; 6) I had not tested their ability to use the information in real life situations.

Over the years, I have seen many lawyer-teachers teach paralegal students in an inappropriately theoretical manner and express profound disappointment and exasperation when the students fail to achieve the level of mastery of the subject which the teacher had desired. I have also seen professionals who are experts in their fields fall into the same trap. Because we have not been students for so many years, we have lost touch with the abilities of students.

The solution to this is three-fold and easy to apply to each new class:

1) Get a feeling for your class from the administration. What is their educational background in general? What is their intellect?

2) Talk to the students themselves in class. Where did you go to high school? How much college did you have? What are your goals in this educational program? (Certificate, AA, BA?) What are your goals for this class?

3) Ask the administration what level they expect of your students. The sample lesson plans they will give you may answer some of these questions.

Once you determine who is in your class, teach at a level which will challenge the majority of the class. By standard grading terms this "majority" is the "middle," the 65 - 80% students. Some schools direct the teacher to teach to the highest level - the 90% and above students. While this is something you must do if directed to, if you have a choice, consider how many students will get left behind. Some administrators advocate teaching to the lowest common denominator, but this usually leaves the majority of the class bored. If you teach to the middle, the less well-prepared student will be either very challenged or left behind. If you sense it is the latter, you must offer extra help (and more praise!) to get the less well-prepared student up to speed. The students who are more well-prepared than the middle can be kept challenged with extra projects.

You will know if you are teaching at the appropriate level by watching the students and listening to their questions. Are they interested? Are they participating or are their eyes glazed over? Are they late or frequently absent? Are their questions on point or did they miss the point? Are their questions simplistic or complex? If you look and listen, you will know. Remember Lesson #8: The good teacher listens to the students.

The Rhinoceros in the Classroom: Discipline

No matter how exciting your class may be, you will not be immune from student discipline problems. The extraordinary discipline problem, such as physical violence, should ordinarily be handled by the administration. Although there are some exceptions, in most teaching experiences your job is to contain the problem (or the student) and deliver it to the appropriate administrative authority.

The more pervasive discipline problem, such as whispering and passing notes during class, is your problem. There are as many different ways of handling that discipline problem as there are human emotions. Teachers typically scold: "Would you two stop that!" Alternatively, teachers ridicule: "Aren't you too old for that?" We overreact: "Get out of my classroom!" And we ignore the disruptive behavior altogether, to the dismay of the well-behaved students.

I have experimented for many years with ways to handle these minor disciplinary problems and I am still searching for the panacea. One thing is certain: that discipline problem is a rhinoceros in the classroom and cannot be ignored.

These are some strategies which work:

- separate the offenders

- tell the offender(s) privately to stop the disruptive activity; if it persists, tell the offender(s) in front of the class to stop

- stop class and instruct the entire class on the negative effects of disruptive behavior on the no-risk class setting while looking at or standing behind the offender

- put a student in charge of the disruptive students: "You are the hall monitor"

- deliver your class lesson while standing next to, between, or over the offender(s)

- mark the offenders absent, if there are administrative consequences for missing class

- give the disruptive student a job, not as a reward, but as subtle punishment

Disruptive behavior should be stopped swiftly. Students should be warned about the consequences of their actions and the teacher must follow through with the punishment. Be sure to be even-handed and consistent. Escalate evenly: a private warning; a public warning; in-class punishment; extra outside-class assignment; administrative intervention. Do not act in anger. Check your motive: it should be the best interests of the class and the disruptive student.

Quick List for Dealing with Difficult Students

1. angry student?
   support, not attack
   focus the student on the real target
   questions, not statements or demands
   offer suggestions for dealing with the real
       target
   encourage a positive attitude in your
       classroom
   invite the student to not attend class with
       hostility
   discipline the student in accordance with
       school policies

2. delay, depersonalize, deflect that hostile
   question

3. motivate the poorly motivated with "special"
   treatment

4. counsel and find resources for the poorly
   prepared student

5. ask the administration for help when necessary

6. adjust for different learning levels

7. don't ignore that rhinoceros

Exams

Developing the Exam

Consider the following five factors when you are developing exams for your class:

1. students' level of mastery of the information at the beginning
2. students' intellectual endowment
3. level of effort
4. progress of the students
5. the ability to succeed at the educational level

Although some of your students will be extraordinarily intelligent and well-prepared for your class, the exam should be geared to the middle of the class. If you make your exam too easy, most of the students will receive A's and this will probably not be in accord with the administration's wishes. If the exam is too difficult, most of the students will receive failing grades and this will probably not be in accord with the administration's wishes. Ordinarily the goal, as discussed below, is to achieve a bell curve where the bulk of the class receives a C grade or better.

Types of Exams

Essay exams are a wonderful way to test the depth and breadth of the students' knowledge, but grading is time-consuming and necessarily subjective. Essay exams give more students more opportunities to be correct, however, and are more in line with the no-risk classroom. Because it is important for students to have good written communication skills, most teachers emphasize the importance of essay exams. Don't forget to be creative when you are writing an essay exam. A simple, boring exam question with Able, Baker and Charlie as the actors in Whiteville can be made more interesting with Argg, Bleeb and Crabby on the Planet Zerg.

Some subjects are better tested in true/false, short answer or multiple choice questions. After years of struggling with grading essay exams in ethics, I changed to multiple choice for one simple reason: I cannot grade someone else's ethics. Some questions are easy to grade: can a paralegal have a business card in this state or not?" Those questions, however, are better asked in true/false or short answer form. The essay question issues: "what do you do when you see someone else committing an unethical act?" contain too much personal choice for traditional grading but are wonderful hypotheticals for class discussion.

The other good thing about short answer, true/false and multiple choice is that you are less likely to have arguments with the students about the grade. The answer is either the one you were looking for or not. Multiple choice questions are not necessarily easy to create so the new teacher should try to get some which have already been tested. If you make up some yourself, beta-test them with some other students so that you can work out the bugs before you give them to your class. Otherwise, you will have those arguments about the "correct answer."

Don't forget that different examination techniques are available to you, such as oral exams, take-home exams, and exam-projects. The object of testing is to find out what the students have learned, how much they have progressed, not to punish them. Before doing anything too creative, however, you should check with your administration to make sure that they do not have a conflicting policy about exam techniques.

Before the Exam

Tell the students the topics to be tested, the format of the test, and what materials they should review. Will you be testing only from the reading? Consider having an open book exam. Students will often spend so much time reading the book, writing in the margins and tabbing and indexing the textbook pages that they will actually learn more than they would learn studying for a closed book exam.

Consider having an exam-review class where you can paint the "big picture" of your class and reinforce the core topics. Encourage your students to "study" and review their notes before this review class so that they can ask those questions they kept meaning to ask and the ones they didn't know they had. You may invite them to write down their questions and give them to you before this review class so that you can focus your review on the topics where there are frequently asked questions. This technique also gives you insight into where your instruction may have been unclear.

If at all possible, institute an open-door policy for your students. They may not come to see you at all during the semester, but they will be standing in line outside your door before the exam.

Administering the Exam

You should find out before the semester begins what responsibilities you have with respect to administering exams. Some schools have proctors who administer exams; some schools expect you to do it. A proctor is often preferable because the students usually will not ask that person questions about the substance of the exam whereas if you are present, all sorts of questions become "fair game." If you will be proctoring your own exams, set out the ground rules before you begin: "I will not answer any substantive questions," or whatever you think is appropriate. Think about the student who will ask you: "Well, what if the answer is kinda true and kinda false?" After awhile, you will think that you have heard them all, but you have not.

Don't think that you should sit at the front of the room and read the newspaper while your students are taking the exam. Walk around the room. Look to see what may be written on the desk top or on someone's arm. Appear interested in finding a cheater and you are less likely to find one. If you do find one, this is a good time to call on the administration for assistance. The one time I found a student cheating, I quietly invited him into the hall and then to the dean's office. It didn't surprise any of the students when he did not return to class - ever.

Grading the Exam

Before you begin to teach, you should review any school policies about what number grade equals what letter grade. At one school an 88% may be a B+ while at another a C-. Information about grading policies is usually in the faculty handbook. What the students are told about grading policies is usually in the student handbook or catalog. You should have all of the available information.

If your administration has given you rules on grading, of course you should follow them. If not, consider grading on a "natural bell curve." A natural bell curve is a curve that is ordinarily created by a class of over 20 students who take the same exam of 100 questions. It will curve from the lowest grade to the highest grade with the bulk of the grades falling in the center of the curve.

8

6   •   •

            •   •

4

      •   •

2

   •   •

60 62 64 66 68 70 72 74 76 78 80

In the above example, the exam had 50 questions worth 2 points each for a total of 100 points. The exam was given to a class of 30 students. One student received a 62%, 1 student an 80%. Six students received 70's and 72s. Three students received 66's and 76's; 5 students received 68's and 74's. This created a traditional natural bell curve where the bulk of the students received a solid "C" score.

The same exam administered to a different group of 30 students produced a "double bell."

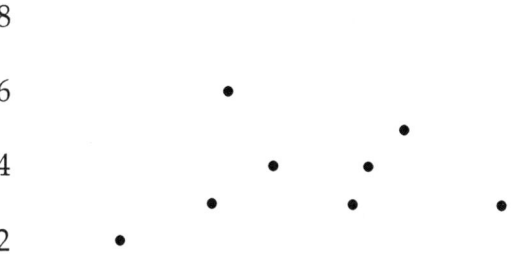

Because the double bell resulted in too many students receiving a "D" grade, my solution was to move both curves up the scale.

```
8

6              •
                      •
4          •      •
        •      •        •
2     •
   60 62 64 66 68 70 72 74 76 78 80 82
```

While I was teaching this class, I noted that there were two "groups" of students on different intellectual levels, but I did nothing about changing the level of my teaching. I did not try to bring the lower group up to the level of the other group. I later adjusted the grades to make up for what I felt was lacking in my approach to the lower-grades group of students. Moving both of the curves up the scale ensured that the students with higher scores were not penalized.

Your exam should have enough questions to test all of the core topics covered in your class. It should also have enough questions so that the grading is fair. In other words, if you give one exam with 10 multiple choice questions, you risk some students receiving very low grades. You might also want to consider using fill-in-the-blank of short answer quesions if your students do not do well with multiple choice questions.

If you are using new exam questions, read all of the exam answers before beginning to mark wrong answers. If your answer was B but everyone in the class answered C, you might want to change your answer or throw out the question. Perhaps the question could be interpreted in more than one way. (This is why your questions should be beta-tested before you use them on your students.) Perhaps you mis-spoke in class and gave the wrong information.

If you toss out the question, you can either recalculate the grades based on fewer questions, or you can give all of the students credit for the right answer so that you don't have to rework the math. In other words, if you started with 25 questions, each right answer is worth 4 points (on 100% scale). If you now have 24 questions, each right answer is worth 4.1666 points. If you don't like math, take the easy road. If the question was badly written, it's the drafter's fault. Give the students 4 points credit for a bad question and continue to count each question as worth 4 points.

Another popular grading method is the "point system." Again, you should tell your students at the beginning of the class how the grading system works. Project A is worth 10 points; pop quizzes worth 5 points each; the midterm has 20 potential points, etc., which all add up to 100. At the end of the course, then, it is a simple matter to add up the points and assign a grade.

You should put comments on the exam, especially if you have tested in essay form. "Good!" in the margin is a concession for the student who may have gotten a grade lower than anticipated. "This is backwards" may be all the explanation the student needs to understand the lower grade. Whatever you write in the margin, your comments should be polite, respectful, sincere and kind. Sarcasm and angry comments will not be appreciated and the student will learn nothing from them.

Mark the exams legibly. If possible, have someone review them for any errors you may have made.

Many teachers have a personal policy which is announced to adult students at the beginning of each new term: Grades will not be changed except for clerical or mathematical errors. In other words, if all of the essays have been graded and yours received a 65%, that grade will not be changed Doing so would necessitate re-reading all of the essays to see where yours fit compared to the others. On the other hand, if the right answer was A and you marked A but the teacher mistakenly marked it as a wrong answer, or if the teacher added the points incorrectly, that grade will be changed. (Having failed to announce this policy for one class, I spent the rest of the semester re-reading essays. Even the student whose essay received a very high grade wanted me to re-read it for points he thought I had missed.) However, if your administration has a policy on this issue, you must follow that policy.

Review the Exam

The point here is learning, so if possible, make the test a learning experience for your students. Consider giving the exam the week before the last week of class so that you have time to review the exam and talk about the answers.

Keep in mind that the students regard their exam scores as their achievements, their goals. Even though you believe that the ultimate goal is to learn self-direction, self-determination, self-control, self-evaluation, self-esteem and critical thinking, the student sees different immediate goals: getting into a good college, going to graduate school, or getting a good job.

Exam review, then, must be consistent with all of the lessons which you have learned in this book: be polite, respectful, sincere, kind, cheerful and fair; show the student how to learn from the exam; be confident in your answers; give praise for the correct answer and for effort; listen and give the students the opportunity to defend their positions.

As you review the exam with your students, make note of the questions they did not understand or which could be worded more clearly.

Grades are confidential. Do not reveal any student's grade without prior permission from the student. Do not make the mistake of thinking that the student with the highest grade wants that grade revealed.

Never publicly criticize a student for a low grade. Although you may be disappointed in a student, do not express that disappointment for the purpose of embarrassing a student. In all of my years of teaching, I have never seen embarrassment work as a positive motivator.

Self Assessment Test:
Do You Really Want To Teach?

The following questions are offered as one way of determining if you are prepared to teach and if you truly want to teach. Grade each answer on the scale of 1 to 5 (5 is the highest). Obviously, the higher your score, the better teacher you will be.

Before class begins

1. Have I mastered the subject matter which I will teach?
2. Am I aware of the current state of my subject?
3. Have I organized each lesson and how each lesson fits with the others?
4. Have I clearly defined the instructional objective for each lesson plan?
5. Have I selected appropriate instructional materials for each lesson to make them more interesting?
6. Have I prepared the lessons at the appropriate level for this class?
7. If you have been teaching for awhile: Have I updated my teaching notes?

In class

8. Do I review the previous classwork before beginning the new class?
9. Do I use a variety of teaching methods?
10. Do I use a variety of teaching materials?
11. Do I frequently ask questions that encourage participation?
12. Do I frequently ask questions that encourage comprehension, analysis, synthesis and evaluation?
13. Do I praise students when they show progress?
14. Do I explain tasks and assignments clearly?
15. Do I relate the lesson to real life?
16. Am I able to hold the interest of the class?
17. Do I know and use the students' names?
18. Is my choice of words on an appropriate level?
19. Do I sound enthusiastic about my topic?
20. Do I avoid embarrassing students?
21. Do I allow all students to be heard?
22. Do I respect students' confidentiality?
23. Do I forgive?
24. Am I courteous?
25. Am I tactful when the student gives an incorrect answer?
26. Do I cultivate my voice to be pleasant, clear and forceful?
27. Am I open to suggestions?
28. Am I punctual?
29. Am I poised and at ease when teaching?

30. Do I have fun when I teach?
31. Do I look for ways to make learning meaningful (or am I just going through the motions)?

Exams

32. Do my tests contain a variety of questions?
33. Do my tests require both critical and creative thinking?
34. Do my students know what to expect on tests?
35. Do I promptly grade and return tests?
36. Do I grade evenly?
37. Do I grade all of the papers together so that they are compared against each other?
38. Do I grade anonymously?
39. Do I grade with ease or is it a chore?
40. Do I grade with learning in mind.

Your score: _____

Doonesbury

BY GARRY TRUDEAU

Some Final Thoughts

Whatever occupation you have chosen should be fun. This isn't a dress rehearsal. I enjoy teaching. I sometimes tell people that I live to teach. If you love teaching, your students will love learning. If you have fun, they will have fun and, as a consequence, they will learn and retain more information.

I encourage you to be a good teacher, a well-liked, self-confident teacher. I encourage you to have fun teaching.

Ten Lessons for Getting an A+ in Teaching

#1   The good teacher is polite, respectful, sincere, kind, cheerful and fair.

#2   The good teacher shows the student how to learn.

#3   The good teacher is self-confident.

#4   The good teacher is well-liked.

#5   The good teacher sets fair goals, praises progress and rewards the students who try.

#6   The good teacher gives the student an opportunity to express views and defend positions.

#7   The good teacher is prepared for the first class and every class thereafter.

#8   The good teacher listens to the students.

#9   The good teacher is honest.

#10   The good teacher is creative.

If you would like to order a copy of this book for yourself or someone who is or wants to be a good teacher, send a $15.00 check made payable to Marlen Hill Publishing to:

Marlen Hill Publishing
2222 Foothill Blvd. #E314
La Cañada, CA 91011-1456

and include your name and address. We'll send your book by first class mail.

You can call us at 818/957-8623.
You can fax us at 818/957-8627.
You can reach us by email at orethics@aol.com

If you like forms, you can reach us that way, too.

I enclose my check for $15.00

_____
Name

_____
Address

_____
Address

_____
City, State, Zip

_____
Phone